OCEANS

KINGFISHER

NEW YORK

KINGFISHER
LONDON & NEW YORK

Text and design copyright © Toucan Books Ltd. 2012
Based on an original concept by Toucan Books Ltd.
Illustrations copyright © Simon Basher 2012

Published in the United States by Kingfisher,
175 Fifth Ave., New York, NY 10010
Kingfisher is an imprint of Macmillan Children's Books, London.
All rights reserved.

Consultant: Dr. Frances Dipper

Designed and created by Basher www.basherbooks.com
Text written by Dan Green

Dedicated to Dave (master chicken), Ness, and Leela

Distributed in the U.S. and Canada by Macmillan,
175 Fifth Ave., New York, NY 10010

Library of Congress Cataloging-in-Publication
data has been applied for.

ISBN: 978-0-7534-6822-7

Kingfisher books are available for special promotions and premiums.
For details contact: Special Markets Department, Macmillan,
175 Fifth Ave., New York, NY 10010.

For more information, please visit www.kingfisherbooks.com

Printed in China
9 8 7 6 5 4 3 2 1
1SCHOL/0412/WKT/UNTD/140MA

Note to readers: the website addresses listed above are correct at
the time of going to print. However, due to the ever-changing nature
of the Internet, website addresses and content can change. Websites
can contain links that are unsuitable for children. The publisher cannot
be held responsible for changes in website addresses or content or for
information obtained through a third party. We strongly advise that
Internet searches should be supervised by an adult.

CONTENTS

Introduction
Oceans

Welcome to the Big Blue—an endless expanse of water that covers most of planet Earth. A million mysteries lurk within these murky depths: creatures living here have to prevent salt from drying out their bodies; there's light for only the first 330–650 ft. (100–200m); temperatures plummet beneath the waves; pressure rises with depth; and sound travels great distances. Yep, this is one weird watery realm.

The most recent tally of all ocean life counted 230,000 species, with at least four times that still awaiting discovery. Your guide to this alien environment is Captain Jacques Cousteau (1910–1997). This Frenchman was an eccentric and pioneering explorer, scientist, filmmaker, author, and co-inventor of the Aqua-Lung (phew!). He made 120 TV documentaries and wrote more than 50 books—his work revealed the hidden underwater world. Jacques was one of the first to think about how humans can harm ocean life and what we can do to protect this eyeball-achingly amazing environment. The ocean is so vast that this book can only dip a toe beneath the surface, but what are you waiting for? Come on in—the water's lovely!

Jacques Cousteau

CHAPTER 1
Water World

Our planet is very special. It's the only one in the entire solar system that has liquid water on its surface. In fact, almost three-fourths of this mighty orb is covered in oceans and seas. It makes you wonder who decided to call it *Earth* in the first place, since anyone can see that it's mostly water! So take this rare opportunity to meet the wet, wild Water World crew. You'll encounter mountains taller than anything on dry land, trenches deeper than Mount Everest is high, and mind-blowingly huge plains. And let's not forget the salt-stained captain of them all—Ocean! Just wade this way . . .

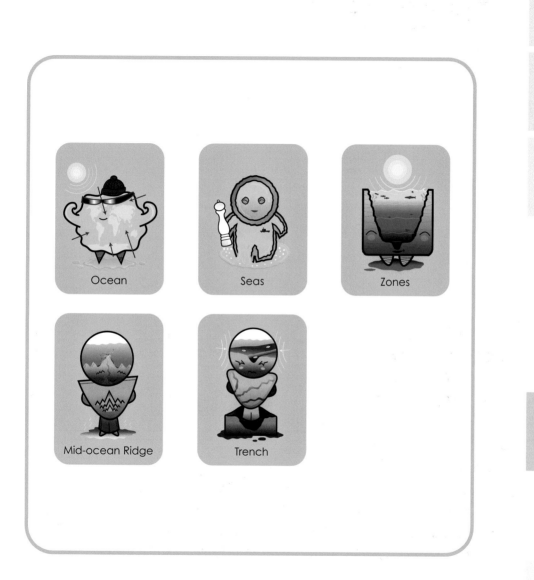

Ocean

Seas

Zones

Mid-ocean Ridge

Trench

Ocean
■ Water World

- ✷ This salty fellow covers 66 percent of Earth's surface
- ✷ Makes up almost three-fourths of the planet's hydrosphere
- ✷ The hydrosphere is all the water in, on, and around the planet

I am the blue-eyed giant, reaching far and wide across the planet's surface. Gaze into my depths and you'll see wonders and mysteries that will blow your mind!

My great volume acts as a sink for the Sun's energy. I soak up its rays, helping keep Earth warm and affecting its climate. My currents drive the world's wind patterns. Though I have only one body, I am divided into five mammoth oceans. The biggest is Pacific, which stretches majestically between the Americas, Asia, and Australia. Atlantic—the saltiest ocean—reaches from Europe to the Americas. Warm Indian Ocean hugs the east coast of Africa up to India, while frigid Southern Ocean wraps around Antarctica. Lastly, small, frozen-over Arctic Ocean sits all a-shiver at the North Pole. Brrr!

- ● Area of all oceans: 139 million sq. mi. (360 million km²)
- ● Volume of all oceans: approximately 312 million cu. mi. (1.3 billion km³)
- ● Average depth of the oceans: 12,435 ft. (3,790m)

Ocean

Seas
■ Water World

* Large areas of salt water connected to the ocean
* Can be completely cut off from the ocean (e.g., Caspian Sea)
* These bodies include gulfs, inlets, passages, and bays

Ahoy there! We are Ocean's little friends. Our boots may be smaller and take less to fill, but we're an important part of Earth's fascinating saltwater story.

The difference between us and Ocean is that we are often surrounded by land (although almost always with a channel to our expansive pal). Our names suggest adventure and romance. Take Celebes, in the western Pacific, with its stunning coral reefs and notorious pirates, or North Atlantic Sargasso—the only sea with no land coasts. Surrounded on all sides by swift Atlantic currents, Sargasso's water is calm, deep blue, and crystal clear. Migrating eels journey here to lay their eggs far below the abundant floating seaweed that also shelters young turtles from predators on the prowl.

● Largest sea: Philippine Sea—surface area: 1,999,145 sq. mi. (5,177,762 km²)
● Proportion of Earth's biomass in the oceans: more than 90%
● In casual speech, the terms *ocean* and *sea* are often used interchangeably

Seas

Zones
■ Water World

☀ Marine environments found at different depths in the ocean
☀ Light, water temperature, and water pressure vary per zone
☀ Some form of life can be found in each of the zones

As well as covering area, Ocean also has depth, and that's where we come in. From surface to floor, we change in character the lower we go.

At the top is the sunlit zone. Sufficient light to allow plants to thrive penetrates about 330–500 ft. (100–150m), which means that 90 percent of all ocean life either resides or feeds here. Below this, the twilight zone has the merest hint of blue light. It's extremely cold and the water pressure is crushing. No plants live here, just hungry carnivores. Lower still, the midnight zone stretches to the near-freezing muddy plains of the ocean floor, home to bottom feeders and witching-hour predators. Finally, there's the impressively deep abyssal zone—up to 19,700 ft. (6,000m)—and the hadal zone, where Trench plunges way down, as low as you can go.

● Sunlit zone (AKA epipelagic zone): 0–650 ft. (0–200m)
● Twilight zone (AKA mesopelagic zone): 650–3,300 ft. (200–1,000m)
● Midnight zone (AKA bathypelagic zone): 3,300–13,100 ft. (1,000–4,000m)

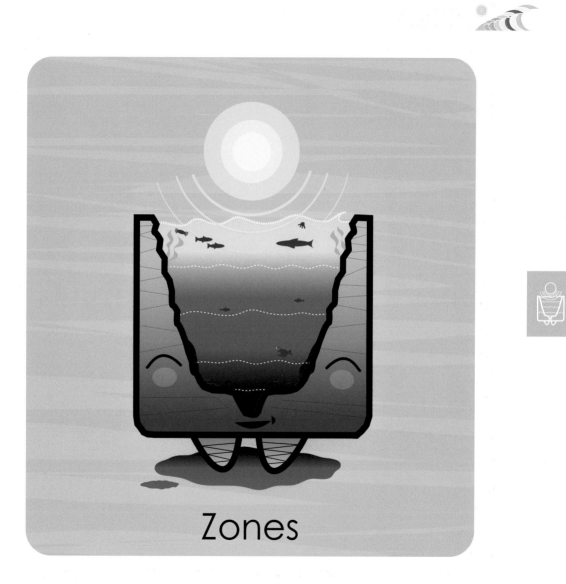

Zones

Mid-ocean Ridge

■ Water World

- ❋ A chain of young mountains that form new ocean floor
- ❋ Longest known mountain range in the universe
- ❋ Tall peaks (seamounts) can grow to form mid-ocean islands

Tall and broad of shoulder, I have underwater peaks that dwarf those on land. Seamounts rear up from my ridges, sometimes breaking the surface to form islands and reefs. My ranges are connected to one another, and I have a very unique skill. Hot and volcanic, I pump out lava to make new ocean crust as part of a process that slowly pushes the continents apart.

Mid-ocean Ridge

- ● Total length of mid-ocean ridge mountain chains: more than 40,000 mi. (65,000km)
- ● Thickness of ocean crust: 0.6–1.2 mi. (1–2km)
- ● Tallest mountain: Mauna Kea, Hawaii, rising 33,474 ft. (10,203m) from ocean floor to summit

Trench
Water World ■

* Deepest, darkest, and coldest part of the ocean
* Huge ditches where ocean crust is dragged back into Earth
* Only three submersibles have ever been this deep

Trench

I am the lowest of the low, a ditch marking where Earth has dragged the ocean floor down into its hungry interior. My deep gullies and fissures plunge suddenly and steeply, thousands of feet below the ocean floor. Because of my head-crushing pressures and water temperatures barely above freezing, humans know more about the surface of the Moon than they do about me.

● Ocean's deepest point: 35,840 ft. (10,924m)—Challenger Deep, Marianas Trench
● Height of Mount Everest: 29,029 ft. (8,848m)
● Proper name for the trench zone: hadal zone

CHAPTER 2
Ocean Motion

With most of the planet covered in sloshy, slippery water, this is a world in motion. Wave transports energy across the oceans as seawater is pushed here and there by the wind. It is here that you'll find Tidal Current trying out a few turbulent tricks. Meanwhile, the Moon pulls Earth's surface toward it, creating two bulges as it orbits, and these force moonstruck Tide to rise and fall. Of course, the big player in this great game is Ocean Current. By shifting warm water around the planet, this stirrer and mixer of vast water masses also drives the world's Weather Systems. What a com-"motion"!

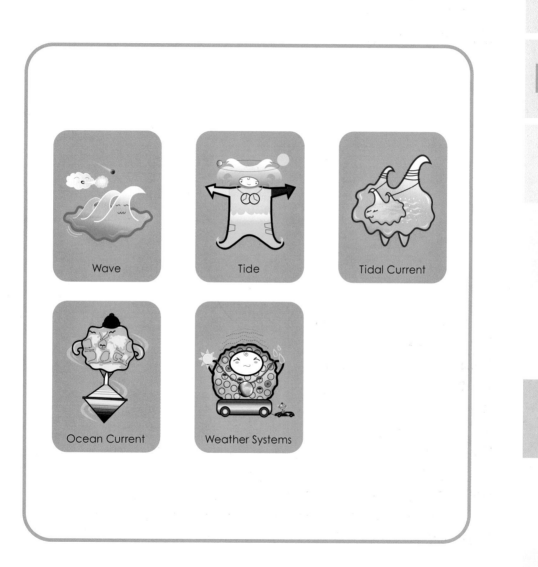

Wave

Tide

Tidal Current

Ocean Current

Weather Systems

Wave
▪ Ocean Motion

☀ An energy surge that travels through water
☀ Wind-generated waves batter coastlines relentlessly
☀ Tsunamis are killer waves that are not generated by wind

I'm the lion of the seas. Shaking my mane and roaring out loud, I come crashing down on beaches and cliffs around the world. Life for me is full of ups and downs, but all in all, I'd say it is pretty *swell*!

Most of the time, I am created by the wind. The friction of air against the surface transfers energy from the wind to the water and starts making the surface bob up and down. I move as a pulse *through* the water rather than taking any of it with me . . . until I hit the shore, that is. Surfers ride my "breakers"—totally bodacious! Tsunamis are my most terrifying form. Generated by underwater earthquakes, landslides, explosions, or falling meteorites, these monster waves travel huge distances, almost invisibly, wreaking destruction wherever they hit land.

● Highest-ever measured storm wave: 95.5 ft. (29.1m)—as tall as a ten-story building
● Biggest tsunami wave: 1,706 ft. (520m) (Lituya Bay, Alaska, 1958)
● A rubber duck moves in circular loops on a wave, with little forward motion

Wave

Tide
■ Ocean Motion

☀ This in-and-out fellow's having a love affair with the Moon
☀ Lunar gravitation attraction causes sea levels to rise and fall
☀ Most places have two high tides and two low tides every day

I'm a bit of a lunatic! As the Moon passes overhead, the water in the ocean feels a tug toward it. That's gravity. In fact, the whole planet feels this force of attraction, but since water is freer to move than land, it is pulled this way and that and sloshes around the planet a little.

At high tide, the water level at the coast rises. Harbors and estuaries fill, waves break closer to the shore, and tidal surges, called bores, race up river channels against the normal direction of flow. At low tide, harbors and estuaries empty, waves break farther out, mud flats are exposed, rock pools form, and seashore life is left shivering in the sun. Spring tides happen whenever the Sun and Moon line up. The extra pull that this creates means that the tides are exceptionally high.

● Biggest recorded tidal range: 70.9 ft. (21.6m) (Bay of Fundy, Canada)
● Spring tide: approximately 20% higher than normal
● Neap tide (alternates with spring tide): approximately 20% lower than normal

Tide

Tidal Current
■ Ocean Motion

- ☀ Strong rush or race of water at, or just below, the surface
- ☀ Its backdrafts, swirls, and eddies make swimming dangerous
- ☀ Often occurs at beaches when the tide turns

I am a devious trickster and thoroughly dangerous to know. I have a bunch of nasty pranks up my sleeve, and I'm *currently* figuring out a way to drag you down.

I have a mind of my own, often rushing in channels of swift-flowing water. I love to go against the flow. Undertow is the dragback of a wave, powerful enough to knock you off your feet. A rip current is a surface race, caused when water is pushed sideways along the shore by more waves breaking behind it. This water rushes back to sea through channels, flattening the incoming waves. It makes the sea look calm, but really it's deadly and can whisk you away from safety. My meanest form is the maelstrom, a wild whirlpool that can suck objects deeper than 330 ft. (100m) below the waves and pull them along the ocean floor.

- ● World's strongest whirlpool: Saltstraumen (Norway)
- ● Skookumchuck: a powerful tidal rapid at a river mouth
- ● On average, rip currents are more deadly than lightning, hurricanes, and tornadoes

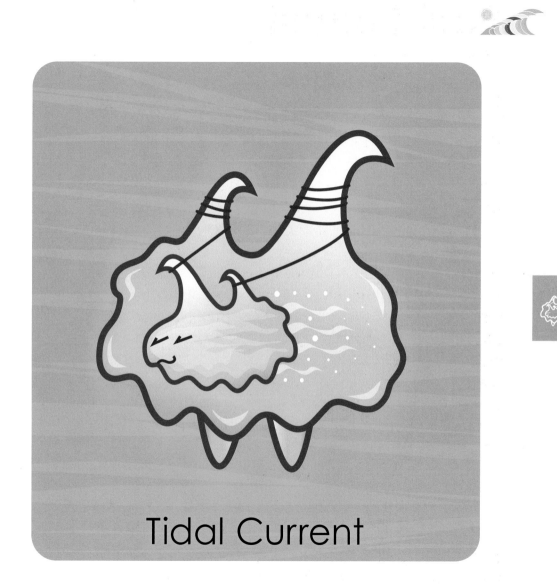

Tidal Current

Ocean Current
■ Ocean Motion

- ☀ Large-scale movement of huge masses of ocean water
- ☀ Called a gyre, there are five of these mammoths in total
- ☀ These vast water loops are driven by the planet's rotation

Wimpy Tidal Current is little more than a stirrer compared with me. When it comes to moving water around, I send it all over the world! You got it, baby—I'm a prime mixer.

With names like North Atlantic Ocean Gyre and Indian Ocean Gyre, I may sound a little dull, but don't you believe it. Driven by Earth's spin, I swirl around in huge, closed loops, speeding ships on their way. Meanwhile, my deeper self gets busy swirling seawater below the surface. Differences in temperature and density drive deep-water currents that bring warmth to polar seas (think Gulf Stream). When these deep waters surface, they bring nutrients up from the depths and provide rich feeding grounds for sea life. These creatures use my swift submarine highways to travel the oceans speedily.

- Unit of measurement: Sverdrup (Sv); 1 Sv = 35,314,662 cu. ft. (1 million m³) seawater per second
- Largest ocean current: Antarctic Circumpolar Current (125 Sv)
- Global ocean conveyor belt: another name for deep-water currents

Ocean Current

Weather Systems
■ Ocean Motion

☀ Movers and shakers that help regulate the global climate
☀ Aid the movement of warm water around the planet
☀ Trade winds carry dust from Africa as far as the Caribbean

Ocean Current and I are coupled together like a car and a trailer, but sometimes it's difficult to know who's doing the pushing and who's pulling!

At the equator, trade winds blow westward, set in motion by the warming Sun and deflected by Earth's rotation. These winds move ocean water around, and together they create my climate patterns, which affect entire regions of the planet. But I'm also driven by Ocean Current: for example, the flow of warm water northward from the tropics is one of the reasons why the North Pole is warmer than the South Pole. Elsewhere, a rise in temperature of the surface waters in the Pacific Ocean creates El Niño episodes about every five years—effectively a reversal of the normal weather cycle.

● Monsoon rain: up to 394 in. (10,000mm) (Indian subcontinent: June–September)
● Average duration of a cyclone: one week
● El Niña: the counterpart to El Niño, bringing lower-than-normal sea temperatures

Weather Systems

CHAPTER 3
Shoreline Gang

The shallow-water zones surrounding Earth's landmasses are a mere drop in the ocean's total volume, but they supply more than 90 percent of our seafood. Young fish stay here until they're big enough to venture out into open water. Closer in, the shore is licked by waves and washed by tides to create a range of different habitats—from sandy beaches, rocky shores, and cliffs to vast mud flats and mangroves. This place is teeming with creatures who are submerged one moment and stranded without water the next. Take a look in any rock pool and you'll find a very special crew scurrying away from you!

Seaweed

Seashells

Sea Slug

Sea Anemone

Sea Urchin

Prawn

Barnacle

Crab

Lobster

Sea Horse

Mudskipper

Marine Iguana

Dugong

Shore Birds

Seaweed

■ Shoreline Gang

- ✳ Large red, green, and brown algae, a different class of plants
- ✳ The biggest seaweed—kelp—forms vast underwater forests
- ✳ As a source of iodine, seaweed keeps many illnesses at bay

We may be your typical marine vegetation, but there's nothing common or ordinary about us! Although some of us are classified as plants, most of us strive to be different.

Yes, we have parts that look like leaves, stems, and roots, and *like* many plants, we use our flat areas to get energy from the Sun via photosynthesis. But *unlike* most plants, we take in nutrients directly from water through our skin—our roots just help us hang on to rocks. Some of us are leathery toughies—gnarly, because we have to endure hours out of the water, crackling in the blistering sunlight. Others have gas-filled bags to keep them afloat (they're a buoyant bunch). In search of sunlight, we anchor almost anywhere. Unlike you, we prefer to sunbathe on rocky shores rather than sandy beaches— hey, we all need something solid to cling on to!

- ● Largest seaweed: giant kelp—fronds up to 200 ft. (60m) long
- ● Growth spurts: giant kelp—up to 20 in. (50cm) per day
- ● Popular uses: sushi, salad, soup, and agar (food thickener)

Seaweed

Seashells

■ Shoreline Gang

☀ A huge range of animals that fall into three main groups
☀ None of these little critters has a skeleton
☀ They make a protective shell in one or two pieces

You may call us homebodies, but we're sensible types who like a little insurance. Just to make sure, we protect our soft bodies within the confines of a hard shell.

We're a diverse bunch that includes brachiopods (lampshells), bivalves (clams and mussels), and gastropods (snails). Walk along any shoreline and, just beneath the waves or in sparkling rock pools, you'll see clinging limpets, grazing periwinkles, jet-propelled scallops, oysters nursing precious pearls, creeping snails, and all sorts of clams, cockles, and mussels. Brachiopods and bivalves live attached to rocks or buried in sand and feed by filtering out food particles from the salty water. Meanwhile, gastropods prefer to graze on algae on rocks or hunt down their prey as they go about their own business.

● Largest clam: giant clam—up to 55 in. (140cm) long
● Boring speed of a shipworm: 6 in. (15cm) of wood in under a year
● Chemical formula of shell: $CaCO_3$ (calcium carbonate)

Seashells

Sea Slug
■ Shoreline Gang

★ A relative of the sea snail with no shell or internal skeleton
★ One of several species of picky eaters with restricted diets
★ Largest and most diverse forms found in warm, shallow waters

Dressed to impress, I rock with the wildest patterns and colors—the more mind-bending, the better. You dig me? A hard shell is just a hassle for me—it cramps my style— so I shrug it off when I become an adult.

I cruise the ocean floor, using my tentacles to touch, taste, and sniff out my prey. I'm something of a specialist in the food department. Collectively, sea slugs eat anything— spiky sponges, stinging hydroids, and squishy sea squirts —but each species favors the same one or two of these delights, day in, day out. I particularly like sea anemones. Their stinging cells pass through my gut wall, and I pop them out of my back for instant protection. Well, when you're as easy to spot and as vulnerable as I am, you have to be clever to avoid becoming someone else's lunch.

● Scientific name: Nudibranchia
● Adult size: 0.8–24 in. (2–60cm) in length
● Distribution: worldwide/all oceans

Sea Slug

Sea Anemone

■ Shoreline Gang

* ☀ This colorful polyp looks pretty . . . but is actually pretty nasty!
* ☀ A small invertebrate that can split itself in two
* ☀ Stays fixed in one spot but can shuffle away if it needs to

Hello, petal! I'm called a "sea flower," but you don't want to start sniffing me! My gently swaying tentacles are armed with stinging cells that stab with tiny toxic threads. My poison paralyzes small fish and prawns, which I pull inside to digest. I'm not a threat to all marine life, though. Clown fish are immune to my toxin, and some crabs happily carry me around on their backs.

Sea Anemone

* ● Scientific name: Actiniaria
* ● Size: ranges from less than 0.5 in. (1.25cm) to almost 5 ft. (1.5m) wide
* ● Distribution: coastal waters worldwide, shallow waters, and deep oceans

Sea Urchin

Shoreline Gang ■

✳ This spiky sea creature has a simple internal shell called a test
✳ Related to five-pointed starfish, brittle stars, and sand dollars
✳ *Urchin* comes from the Middle English word for a hedgehog

Sea
Urchin

I'm a bristling spiky ball with see-through "tube feet." I pick my way across rock pools and reefs looking for seaweed, algae, sponges, and even tough barnacles to scrape off and munch on. Beneath my defensive spines and hard armor plates, I'm a star-shaped softy. Looking at me, you'd never guess I was a tasty treat, but sea otters, wolf eels, and humans go crazy for my soft center.

● Typical size range: 1–5 in. (3–12cm) wide
● Largest sea urchin: *Sperosoma giganteum*—13 in. (32cm) wide, on average
● Longest spines: up to 12 in. (30cm) long (long-spined sea urchin)

Prawn

■ Shoreline Gang

- ✳ Ten-legged crustacean, also called the "insect of the sea"
- ✳ Related to shrimp, crabs, crayfish, and lobsters
- ✳ Hangs around rocky areas, close to the ocean floor

You'd think I'd be ready for anything: I have tactile antennae up front; I have five pairs of legs, some with claws; I even wear a helmet on my head, complete with a jagged spear. Yet I twitch and flitter like a nervous wreck. You see, I'm tasty! And while I feed quite peacefully on detritus— not a threat to a soul— my predators often force me to skitter under rocks.

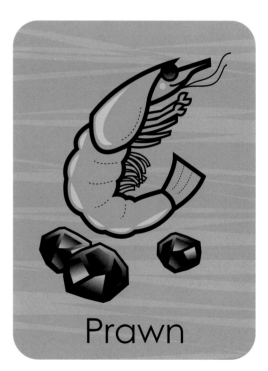

Prawn

- ● Scientific name: Decapoda
- ● Largest prawn: black tiger prawn—up to 14 in. (36cm)
- ● Prawns look similar to shrimp but have longer legs and a different gill structure

Barnacle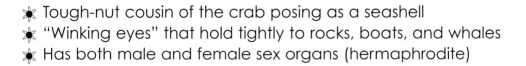

Shoreline Gang ▪

- ✳ Tough-nut cousin of the crab posing as a seashell
- ✳ "Winking eyes" that hold tightly to rocks, boats, and whales
- ✳ Has both male and female sex organs (hermaphrodite)

Barnacle

With a trick stolen from Seashells, I've covered my soft body in a hard shell. I cling to rocks, and my thick top plates clamp shut to lock out predators and keep me from drying out in the sun at low tide. It's a smart system that allows me to live in inhospitable shore zones, where waves are rough. At high tide, I slide my hatches open and stick out my feathery legs to filter food from the water.

- ● Size: 0.2–2 in. (0.5–5cm) wide
- ● Number of known species: more than 1,000
- ● Life span: 5–10 years

 # Crab

■ Shoreline Gang

✳ Sideways mover with ten legs and armor plating
✳ Communicates by drumming or waving its pincers
✳ Related to lobsters, but true crabs tuck their tails underneath

Clickety clack! I'm a hard-nut shoreline scavenger, prizing food out with my snappy claws. There's very little I won't eat. My favorite place is a rocky seashore, where you'll see me scurrying along the water's edge, eyes (literally) on stalks. I'm aware that I'm a tasty fellow, so sometimes I carry Sea Anemone on my back for protection. There's a sting in my tale!

Crab

● Smallest crab: male pea crab—up to 0.2 in. (4mm) wide
● Largest crab: Japanese spider crab—10–13-ft. (3–4-m) leg span
● Distribution: worldwide/all oceans

Lobster

Shoreline Gang ▪

* Crustacean with five pairs of legs, the front three with claws
* An omnivore who mopes around quietly on the ocean floor
* A tasty critter, protected by restrictions on size when caught

Lobster

Unlike hyperactive Crab, I simply am not happy scurrying above the waves. You see, I'm—well—*more upmarket*! Blue blood runs through my veins, thanks to its high copper content. I lead a solitary life, under rocks and in crevices. You might see me marching in (a straight, not sideways) line to egg-laying grounds. If I need to escape, I do it backward, with brisk jerks of my abdomen.

● Heaviest lobster: American lobster—up to 44.4 lb. (20.15kg)
● Swimming speed: up to 16 ft. (5m) per second
● Distribution: worldwide/all oceans

Sea Horse
■ Shoreline Gang

⚹ Pipefish family member who likes to mate under a full moon
⚹ Wears a crown that is as individual as a fingerprint
⚹ The Greek god Poseidon is often depicted riding a sea horse

I'm a funny fish. With my long face, potbelly, and head sunk deep in thought, I look like a tiny underwater professor. And I'm not one for galloping around, either!

In fact, I'm one of the world's slowest swimmers, wrapping my curly tail around a plant when I need to rest. I'm the only fish that swims bolt upright, flitting through fronds of sea meadows and forests, chasing teeny shrimp, baby fish, and plankton. Instead of fishy scales, I have a thin skin that changes color to blend in with wherever I am. Mating for me is a real performance—I dance with my partner, linking tails and twirling around. When the time is right, I show her the empty egg pouch on my belly and she drops her eggs into it. I'm the only male animal in the whole world that can get pregnant!

● Size: from 0.6 in. (15mm) (pygmy sea horse) to 12 in. (30cm) (Pacific sea horse)
● Strangest sea horse: leafy sea dragon, with its leaflike camouflage
● Distribution: shallow, tropical, and temperate waters

Sea Horse

Mudskipper

■ Shoreline Gang

☀ Amphibious fish that breathes through its skin out of water
☀ Can use its strong fins to skip up to 24 in. (60cm) in the air
☀ Escapes predators by resting on tree roots above water

Well, whaddayaknow? Meet Johnny Jumper, a real fish out of water! Looking at my bulging eyes and the frill down my back, you might mistake me for a frog or a lizard. I'm right at home when the tide goes out. No scurrying to rock pools or seaweed for me. No, I'm happy in my mud hole. I skip around using super-pumped-up pectoral fins. With bubbly water in my gills, I'm never out of breath.

Mudskipper

● Average size: 3.7 in. (9.5cm) long
● Best-known species: *Periophthalmus argentilineatus*
● Distribution: tropical mud flats and mangrove swamps

Marine Iguana
Shoreline Gang ■

* The world's only oceangoing lizard
* A gentle herbivore with a mohawk of spines
* Called the "imp of darkness" by naturalist Charles Darwin

Marine
Iguana

My razor-sharp teeth and long claws give me a fierce look, but I'm no devil. I like nothing more than a juicy nibble on seaweed and underwater algae. My stubby snout lets me get up close to rocks to crop that tricky-to-get-to-but-darn-tasty sea veggie, and my tough face is laced with a white salt crust. Hey, when you take in this much salt, why not sneeze some out all over yourself?

● Average size: female—2 ft. (0.6m) long; male—4.3 ft. (1.3m) long
● Maximum diving depth: 33 ft. (10m)
● Coloration: gray-black, with males developing red patches in the mating season

Dugong
■ Shoreline Gang

✳ A large marine mammal also known as a "sea cow"
✳ Related to manatees and elephants
✳ This gentle giant of coastal waters is becoming extinct

They say that sailors used to mistake me for a mermaid. Ha! They must have been at sea too long! I may have lovely smooth brown skin, but I also have floppy dog jowls and a downturned mouth. I'm no looker!

My real interest is sea grass. Fields of this deliciously juicy plant are found in warm, shallow waters, and I spend my time grazing and cruising between pastures. I love the shallows and often stick my head up out of the water for a breath of fresh air. If I need to, I'm able to dive down to 130 ft. (40m). Taking deep breaths from the nostrils on the tip of my muzzle, I slip underwater for up to six minutes at a time. Sadly, my meadows are being lost, and I am hunted or snared in fishnets by mistake. I'm vulnerable to extinction and may soon be gone forever.

● Average size: 9 ft. (2.7m) long
● Oldest dugongs: 70 years old
● Distribution: warm coastal waters from East Africa to Australia

Dugong

Shore Birds

■ Shoreline Gang

☀ Group of wading birds in the intertidal zone
☀ Careful and deliberate hunters, some with very long bills
☀ Seek out all types of burrowing invertebrates

We're a bright bunch of beachcombing birds. Strutting along the seashore, sloshing through wet sand, and sifting through debris, we work the shoreline in crews.

This is not a life for the faint-hearted. It gets pretty chilly, even if you have a nice down undercoat. The rewards are great—delicious wiggly ragworms, juicy mollusks, beach fleas, and the odd sand-coated mole crab. There's nothing we love better than wading across a good mud flat, where the pickings are rich. Hunting techniques vary: we poke and prod the sand with our bills or do a little stone flipping. High-tech nerve endings in our bills help some of us detect prey. Different species have different-length bills, which means that we can plunder the same coastline without eating one another's lunch.

● Smallest shore bird: least sandpiper—5 in. (13cm) tall
● Largest shore bird: Far Eastern curlew—25 in. (63cm) tall
● Species include sandpipers, curlews, sheathbills, snipes, plovers, oystercatchers

Shore Birds

CHAPTER 4
Reef Chillin'

A riot of color, coral reefs play host to some pretty wild scenes. Life is a carnival, with almost one-fourth of the world's marine species either living on reefs or simply chillin' out down there. The reefs themselves are alive—inhabited by tiny coral polyps—and their towering structures provide homes for a bewildering parade of marine life. The entire reef community depends on the health of lovely Coral—a fragile habitat increasingly endangered by environmental change. Corals prefer warm, sunlit waters, but some hardy types try out deep, dark, and cold northern waters (now *that's* chillin'!).

Coral

Sea Fan

Sponge

Starfish

Reef Tenders

Reef Hunters

Moray Eel

Ray

Blue-ringed Octopus

Coral

▪ Reef Chillin'

- ✳ Soft-bodied house-building animals called polyps
- ✳ Their hard, stone houses offer protection from predators
- ✳ Some corals make reefs that can live for thousands of years

We live in high-rise colonies, all crammed in on top of one another. Our white, calcium-carbonate apartments might be a squeeze, but there's always plenty of clear, unpolluted water, good light, and warmth.

What's known as a "coral head" is actually a vast colony of colorful, genetically identical polyps, each only a fraction of an inch (a few millimeters) across. Many hands make light work, and there is no shortage of labor here. Most of us build slowly and steadily, but we are master masons. For proof, just look at the Great Barrier Reef—you can see it from space! We operate a strict one-polyp, one-house policy, with nutrients piped in via a system of canals. We've also teamed up with algae, who take energy from the Sun and provide us with food.

- ● Coral types: massive, branching, columnar, encrusting, and plate
- ● Deepest-living coral: *Lophelia*—9,800 ft. (3,000m)
- ● Largest coral reef: Great Barrier Reef—1,600 mi. (2,600km) long

Coral

Sea Fan

■ Reef Chillin'

☀ Flexible, non-reef-forming coral rooted to a hard surface
☀ This flattened spray of color is related to the sea anemone
☀ Has stinging cells that snare tiny creatures

Fan-tastically elegant and brightly colored, I am the peacock of the sea. But, beware, my flashy whips spell danger for some. Like my cousins Jellyfish, Coral, and Sea Anemone, I'm a stinger. (Why else would they call me Gorgonian, after mythical Medusa, who had biting snakes for hair?) Inhospitable, you might think, but I provide a safe harbor for tiny goby fish and sea horses.

Sea Fan

● Scientific name: Gorgonacea
● Number of species: at least 500
● Distribution: shallow, tropical waters, especially the Caribbean and Indo-Pacific

Sponge
Reef Chillin' ■

- ✳ Structurally, one of the simplest multicellular animals that exists
- ✳ Attaches to hard surfaces and grows into strange shapes
- ✳ Has no stomach, so filters food from the water through pores

Sponge

Chillax, dude! I keep things cool by not being overly complicated. What more do you need in life than a body full of holes and channels awash with lovely cold water helped along by microscopic hairs? I use currents to bring me food particles suspended in the water. I also have an awesome superpower— I can regenerate my body if it gets chopped into pieces. Simple pleasures . . .

- ● Scientific name: Porifera
- ● Number of species: about 5,000
- ● Volume of water filtered by a sponge per day: up to 20,000 times its own volume

Starfish
■ Reef Chillin'

* Brightly colored, star-shaped invertebrate echinoderm
* A sea-floor dweller with arms called rays and protective spines
* Around 2,000 species exist, most with five arms

Yep, you guessed it—I'm a total superstar! Devastatingly handsome, I cruise the ocean floor on my tiny tube feet, arms outstretched and on the prowl for tasty tidbits.

A nice mussel, a juicy clam, or a delicious ailing fish— anything too sluggish to escape my slow-motion attack has had it. I scramble on top, spit out my stomach, and begin digesting right away. Eating like this means that I can gobble things that are bigger than my mouth— it's the ultimate out-of-body experience! I may be a no-brainer, but I'm no fool—I have a complex nervous system with a light-detecting "eyespot" at the end of each arm. And if I lose an arm to a predator, I can regrow it. Some species can even regrow an entire body from a dismembered arm. Now that's a *star*-quality trick.

● Largest starfish: sunflower starfish—3-ft. (1-m) arm span
● Greatest number of arms: *Labidiaster annulatus* (up to 50)
● Distribution: worldwide/all oceans

Starfish

Reef Tenders

■ Reef Chillin'

- ✳ An incredibly diverse fish population that inhabits coral reefs
- ✳ These brightly colored critters bristle with defense strategies
- ✳ Built for maneuverability rather than speed

Featuring blinding yellows, deep purples, and winks of electric blue, we are truly a pretty sight. But think again if coral reef spells tropical paradise to you. It's a pitiless world, in which Coral and Sponge battle for territory.

Here on the reef, you need all kinds of poisons and spikes just to get you through the day! Parrotfish keeps algae under control when it crunches Coral with its birdlike beak. In swims butterfly fish, its tweezerlike mouth nipping off little coral polyps like grapes. Clown fish seeks protection from predators by hanging out with stinging Sea Anemone. And cleaners wrasse and shrimp run a valet service for sharks and big fish, scrubbing teeth, trimming back dead scales, and removing parasites. Nice work if you can get it!

- ● Number of coral-reef fish species: 6,000–8,000
- ● Sand produced by parrotfish crunching coral: up to 200 lb. (90kg) per year
- ● Some parrotfish blow a protective cover of slime around themselves at night

Reef Tenders

Reef Hunters

Reef Chillin'

* Merciless predators who terrorize the reef tenders
* Some, like the white-tip reef shark, hunt in packs at night
* Ambush predators are very difficult to spot

Lean, mean, and keen to make a killing on the reef, we are one menacing mercenary mob. Among those to fear are tasseled scorpion fish and frogfish, who melt into the undergrowth waiting to ambush unwitting swimmersby.

Meanwhile, pitiless barracuda patrols the reef edges, its streamlined, torpedo-shaped body allowing for blistering bursts of speed. Blazing out of nowhere, it tears an unwary fish into shreds with its razor-sharp conical teeth. Bigeye trevally is a diligent hunter who forces smaller fish up against the reef, picking off stragglers in the confusion and panic. Sea snake's flattened tail acts as a paddle for chasing after fish and hunting down eel in their hiding places. The most flamboyant of our crew is lionfish—a small dude with a "lion's mane" of defensive spines. Ouch!

* Most venomous fish: reef stonefish
* Largest reef predator: grouper—7.5 ft. (2.3m) long (Costa Rica, 2010)
* Longest sea snake: up to 9 ft. (2.75m) (yellow sea snake)

Reef Hunters

Moray Eel
■ Reef Chillin'

* Snappy character with a long, wiggly body and smooth skin
* A master of camouflage in muddy brown or bright green
* Eats fish, mollusks, crustaceans, and blue-ringed octopuses

I have a long fin running from tip to tail, a quirky narrow head, and a slight bagginess that makes me look like a sock puppet. But I'm no play-time pal—only big hunters such as barracuda or sea snakes will take me on.

I hunt for food at night, but I am also a world-class lurker. Some of my favorite haunts include old pipes and the portholes of sunken ships, where I loiter with my mouth hanging open. Should something tasty pass by, I lunge for it, grasping and biting at it with my razor-sharp teeth. A terrifying second set of jaws in my throat reaches forward to clamp down on prey in my mouth, dragging it into the pit of my stomach. I avoid contact with humans, but I have been known to take a wholesome chunk out of a passing diver—hence my curmudgeonly reputation.

● Smallest moray: Snyder's moray—up to 4.5 in. (11.5cm) long
● Longest moray: slender giant moray—up to 13 ft. (4m) long
● Distribution: tropical and temperate seas worldwide

Moray Eel

Ray
▪ Reef Chillin'

☀ A flatfish with a sting in its tail
☀ Grazes on the ocean floor, digging out clams and crabs
☀ Ray stings are tipped with venom and can be fatal

Hi, I'm Ray, a member of the shark family. I have stiff, rubbery cartilage rather than hard bones, and my rough skin is used on the handles of Japanese samurai swords.

To all and sundry, I am a hooded sorcerer with a rippling, winged cloak and a fearsome reputation. In truth, I have a gentle nature; I'm docile and curious. I'm more likely to glide up to you rather than hurt you, to see what you're doing . . . petting you with a fin. The sting? Always the thing about the sting! Sigh. Yes, some of us (but not all) have a whiplike tail armed with a barbed stinger. More like a tail with a tooth . . . with venom glands . . . Nasty, I know, but we all need defense mechanisms. Some of us even give the occasional electric shock, but most of us are happy to cruise peacefully along the seabed.

● Scientific name: Batoidea
● Largest species: giant manta ray—average 20-ft. (6-m) wingspan
● Distribution: coastal warm waters and reefs worldwide

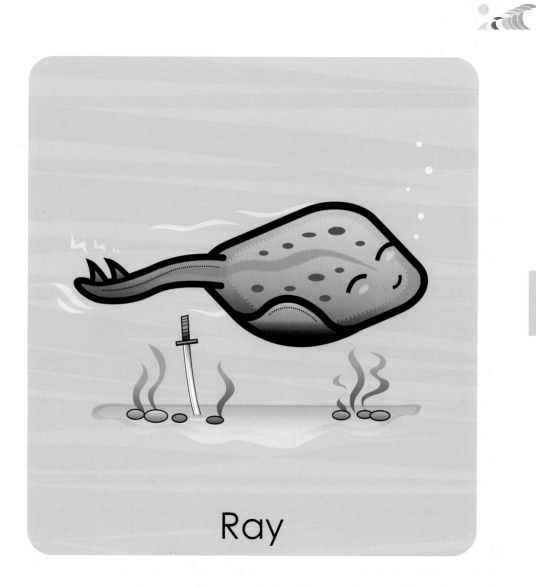

Ray

Blue-ringed Octopus
Reef Chillin'

* Cephalopod family member, cousin to squids and cuttlefish
* One of the world's most venomous animals
* Octopuses have three hearts and blue, copper-rich blood

I'm a killer with enough poison onboard to finish off 26 adult humans and a beak that can easily slice into a finger. There's no cure for my bite: you could be dead within five minutes.

Most octopuses are small—I'm the size of a golf ball with arms. Shy and retiring, I hide away inside empty shells or rock crevices, using my color-changing camouflaged skin to catch crabs, shrimp, and small fish unawares. Like all octos, I travel by jet propulsion, and when in trouble, I shoot out clouds of distracting dark ink. Provoke me and my rings flash electric blue in panic, terror, and rage. This is when you usually spot me, but by then, it's too late!

● Average size: body—2 in. (5cm); arms—4 in. (10cm)
● World's heaviest octopus: North Pacific giant octopus—up to 157 lb. (71 kg)
● Distribution: tidal pools from Japan to southern Australia

Blue-ringed Octopus

CHAPTER 5
Open-water Crew

More than half of the world's surface is open water, far away from the shore and a long way from the ocean floor. Most things live in the top 650 ft. (200m) or so, lit by the sun. They congregate where upwelling currents bring nutrients in from the deep. This is a good place to live, protected from the worst of the Sun's radiation, which can interfere with DNA. There is no fear of drying out, either—temperature extremes that occur on land do not arise here, and creatures are surrounded on all sides by the chemicals and food needed to sustain life. The result is a diverse range of open-water inhabitants. Ready for a dip?

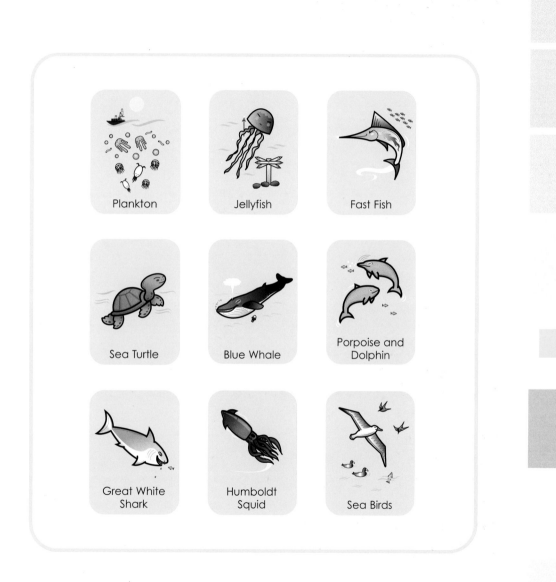

Plankton

Jellyfish

Fast Fish

Sea Turtle

Blue Whale

Porpoise and Dolphin

Great White Shark

Humboldt Squid

Sea Birds

Plankton
Open-water Crew

* Microscopic drifters called phytoplankton and zooplankton
* Burst into life in the spring, turning parts of the ocean green
* Phytoplankton is the ocean's main source of plant food

Green and serene, we are members of an entire world of microscopic plants and animals that float free in the ocean. All we need for life is light, clean water, and food.

Some of us are super-tiny plants known as phytoplankton (say "fye-toe-plank-ton"). Soaking up the Sun's rays, we produce half of the world's oxygen. Floating alongside, gorging on our veggie buffet, are billions of microscopic beasts such as jellyfish, crustaceans, snails, squids, and fish larvae. This zooplankton (say "zoe-uh-plank-ton") makes a great snack in itself—it's gobbled up by a host of nightmarish creatures who ascend from the deep after sundown. Together, we attract forage fish, jellyfish, basking sharks, and sea birds, as well as seals, sea lions, and whales. You could say we are the ocean's biggest attraction!

● Smallest plankton: picoplankton—0.0002–0.02mm (bacteria, small protists)
● Largest plankton: megaplankton—0.8–8 in. (2–20cm) (some seaweed and jellyfish)
● Spring bloom: term for rapid growth of phytoplankton as the oceans warm up

Plankton

Jellyfish
Open-water Crew

☀ Free-swimming, brainless wonder—the largest kind of plankton
☀ One of four different classes of related stinging animals
☀ Some tiny fish hide from predators behind jellyfish tentacles

A jelly-belly dancer, I am a silent and deadly menace of the ocean. I float rather than swim, pulsing softly like a heartbeat, going wherever the ocean currents take me.

I am simplicity itself. I don't have a central nervous system, let alone a brain, and I breathe through my skin, so there's no need for complicated gills. I might be 90 percent water, but I'm no drip! My trailing tentacles are lined with spring-loaded, venom-tipped spears that fire into the body of anything that happens to get tangled in them. In some of us, this "curtain of death" is powerful enough to kill a human. Like my photoplankton cousins, I bloom in the right conditions. My microscopic larvae suddenly mature into full-blown jellies, instantly creating a swarm of hundreds of thousands of beautiful blobs.

● Most deadly jellyfish: box jellyfish
● Longest tentacles: lion's mane jellyfish—up to 121 ft. (37m)
● Distribution: worldwide/all oceans

Jellyfish

Fast Fish

Open-water Crew

* Low-friction fish that move like bullets through the water
* Marlins and swordfish swim alone; others, like tuna, form schools
* These guys do everything on the move—even rest!

Ruling the open ocean and built for lightning speed, we are obsessed with streamlining. Just try to catch a glimpse of us as we flit past with a flash and a twinkle.

We are like sleek torpedoes. Our eyes are flush with our bodies, and we have stiff, narrow fins that we can tuck back into hollow slots. Anything that causes drag is out—too many scales, for example. Some of the fastest in our crew—marlins, sailfish, and swordfish—have rapier-like noses that really "slice" through the water. Many of us group together in vast schools. We love to eat herring and need awesome control to catch them as they swirl in the water. We have a line of extra-sensitive cells running down each side of the body, and this keeps us from crashing into one another as we give chase.

● Fastest fish: Indo-Pacific sailfish—bursts of 68 mph (110km/h)
● Tuna migration: about 6,700 mi. (10,800km), from western Atlantic to Mediterranean
● Fastest time taken to cross the Atlantic Ocean: 119 days—bluefin tuna

Fast Fish

Sea Turtle
Open-water Crew

- Marine reptile called a chelonian that can live for 80 years
- The only animal on Earth that is immune to box-jellyfish stings
- Lays eggs by moonlight on beaches

The old lady of the water world, I roam far and wide across Earth's oceans. I'm a peace-loving soul, sadly on the brink of becoming an endangered species.

I breathe air and have to surface to gulp it down, but I'm much more at home in the water. In fact, I go ashore only to lay my eggs. Life as a youngster is terrifying. Hatching on the beach, I have to make it past beady-eyed sea birds to get to the water. Then I have to dodge hungry fish and predatory sharks. A sharp beak and exceptional night vision allow leatherback turtles to live on a diet of jellyfish, while green turtles are content with sea grass and seaweed, and hawksbills favor sponges. I travel great distances, but I'm cold-blooded, so I prefer warmish waters—chillier climes just make me sluggish!

- Largest turtle: leatherback—average shell length 80 in. (200cm)
- Number of eggs in a clutch: 50–200
- Distribution: all oceans except for the Arctic Ocean

Sea Turtle

Blue Whale

Open-water Crew

- ✳ A seagoing mammal, the largest animal ever to have existed
- ✳ Can stay underwater for at least 30 minutes and loves singing
- ✳ Closest relative is the landlubbing hippopotamus

I am the ocean's buried treasure, one of Earth's natural wonders. As big as two school buses and mostly hidden from sight, I am even bigger than the biggest dinosaur!

My heart weighs as much as a car, and each eye is the size of a soccerball! When I exhale at the surface after a long dive, my breath condenses and a steamy spray jets 30 ft. (9m) up into the air! I'm a hungry fellow, and it takes more than a couple of servings of krill to fill my huge belly—in fact, I eat up to 6 tons every day! I simply open wide and gulp. Inrushing seawater pulls in fish and krill, and straining the water out through my big "baleen" mustache leaves them trapped where I can lick 'em off! These truckloads of krill help me build a nice, thick blubber layer to keep me warm. Ain't no barnacles on me . . . oh yeah, there are!

- ● Length: up to 100 ft. (30m)
- ● Average speed: 12 mph (20km/h)
- ● Communication: can hear one another over a distance of up to 1,000 mi. (1,600km)

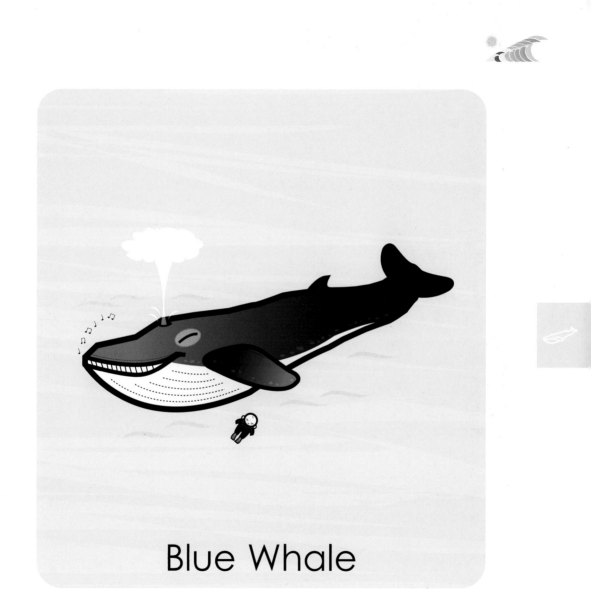

Blue Whale

Porpoise and Dolphin

Open-water Crew

- ✳ Big-brained mammals that live in family groups called pods
- ✳ Move by pumping the tail up and down
- ✳ There are about 40 species of dolphins and six of porpoise

Meet Porpoise and Dolphin, leaping live wires, the movie stars of the ocean show. You can't miss us—we're a jolly pair, always ready to greet you with a little smile.

Behind Dolphin's shapely head and beak is a super-slick brain. No less intelligent, Porpoise has a smoother profile and shorter snout. We're famed for being smart: we locate fish with sonar clicks and ultrasonic beeps, and we talk to one another with clicks and whistles as we speed along. We're always learning new tricks—herding fish by blowing bubbles or hydroplaning on the surface of the water. Speedy Dall's porpoise is the fastest of us all, while a spinner dolphin can turn four times in the air. Flipping fantastic!

- ● Speed of a Dall's porpoise: up to 34 mph (55km/h)
- ● Superpod: a group of more than 1,000 members
- ● Life span: 45–50 years (bottle-nosed dolphin)

Porpoise and Dolphin

Great White Shark

Open-water Crew

* The ocean's largest predatory fish
* Uses its muscle-packed, turbocharged tail to keep swimming
* Takes huge bites with jaws that are not attached to its skull

Swift and deadly, I am loaded with sensory equipment and I'm on the prowl. Oh yeah, mine is a toothy grin that other fish really *don't* want to see!

I have detection abilities that put other animals to shame: super-sharp hearing, an acute electrical sense that can make out another fish's heartbeat, and a nose that senses tiny amounts of blood in the water up to 3 mi. (5km) away. My teeth grow in rows that roll forward as old ones fall out, so I have a constant supply of sparkling new gnashers! Despite this, most people actually survive a shark attack, because my first chomp is always an exploratory nibble. Humans don't taste good, so I rarely come back for the killer bite. My eyes never close, but, boy, do I like to roll them back in their sockets when I go in for the kill!

* Scientific name: *Carcharodon carcharias*
* Largest size: more than 20 ft. (6m) long
* Number of teeth: up to 300

Great White Shark

Humboldt Squid

Open-water Crew

* This speedy character is smarter than the average fish
* Hides out during the day at depths below 1,000 ft. (300m)
* Signals to fellow squids by changing color

I'm a little red devil (or so say Peruvian fishermen), riding the Humboldt Current off the west coast of South America. I travel in gangs of one thousand or more, zipping out of the deep and flashing red and white warnings to my pals.

With short fins and a bullet body, I'm not built for comfort—I'm built for speed. My siphon jets me along rapidly, tail first! I may have a touchy-feely side, but my instinct is to eat first, explore later. Two feeding arms bring food back to my mouth, turning it like corn on the cob while I tear at it with my viciously sharp beak. My gang has even been known to hunt together, "squidnapping" larger animals. If you're diving with me, you need to wear super-tough gear: my razor-edged, serrated suckers might not bring the sort of attention you enjoy!

- Largest Humboldt squid: 5.8 ft. (1.75m) long
- Top speed: more than 15 mph (24km/h)
- Average life span: 1 year

Humboldt Squid

Sea Birds

Open-water Crew

- ☀ Include tubenoses, penguins, boobies, terns, and skimmers
- ☀ Feed at sea but nest in vast colonies on land
- ☀ These globetrotters live longer than most other birds

Caw, caw! We're a squawking bunch of feathered fine diners. We'll go to any lengths to get our daily helping of fish, squids, and shellfish.

You've got your terns and cormorants, sneaky gulls and frigate birds, skuas, guillemots and gannets, pelicans and petrels. Our fishing techniques are diverse—dipping and skimming, dive-bombing, and out-and-out underwater pursuit. Waterproofing is a must, and we all have an oil gland at the tip of our tails that we dip into when we preen. There are some real Olympians among us. The albatross has the longest wingspan of all living birds, while the arctic tern breeds in the Arctic and then flies to the Antarctic over the winter and back again. Sadly, the mighty albatross are the most threatened birds on Earth.

- ● Smallest sea bird: storm petrel—5–10 in. (13–26cm) long
- ● Albatross wingspan: up to 11 ft. (3.4m)
- ● Arctic tern migration: about 50,000 mi. (80,500km) every year

Sea Birds

CHAPTER 6
Deep-down Dandies

This zone and its denizens are shrouded in darkness—it's a place we know less about than the surface of Mars! It's always chilly, even in tropical areas, and the pressure could crush a human skull. A kind of perpetual dandruff of dead plants and animals, called "marine snow," rains down from above. The fish in this bizarre place are small and black, with large mouths, stretchy stomachs, no scales, and flabby muscles. They are not good swimmers and they're not too pretty, but many can do the most bewitching things with lights—flashing to find or communicate with one another in the dark.

Tripod Fish

Anglerfish

Hagfish

Sea Cucumber

Hydrothermal Vent

Tripod Fish
■ Deep-down Dandies

- ✳ Stands on three rays extending from the pelvic fins and tail
- ✳ Almost blind but sensitive to pressure and touch
- ✳ Has both male and female parts (hermaphrodite)

Cruising slowly, I come to rest above the ocean floor on my very long fin rays. Three spindly supports trail wispily behind me when I swim but become stiff enough to keep me in position to feed. Once settled, I turn my face into the current, extending my pectoral fins forward to "feel" for shrimp and plankton, which I snap up as they drift past.

Tripod Fish

- ● Scientific name: *Bathypterois grallator*
- ● Average size: about 12 in. (30cm) long
- ● Tripod fish live on the sea floor at depths of up to 18,400 ft. (5,600m)

Anglerfish

Deep-down Dandies ▪

- ✷ A fishing fish with a glowing "photophore" lure
- ✷ Has an upward-pointing mouth and a very flexible jaw
- ✷ In some species, males attach to, and live off, females

Anglerfish

Someone once asked me how I came to be called the deep-sea anglerfish. Well, I live in the deep sea, I bait my food . . . oh, and I'm a fish! I'm no looker, but my dark, lumpy skin acts as a camouflage in the pitch black. I'm rather flabby and a slow swimmer, so, like many anglers, I hang around a lot. I simply dangle a glowing lure in front of a mouthful of long, curved teeth—and wait!

- ● Scientific name: Lophiiformes
- ● Size: male—up to 1 in. (3cm); female—up to 7 in. (18cm)
- ● Nickname: common black devil

Hagfish

■ Deep-down Dandies

* ✷ Ancient fish, without jaws or real fins
* ✷ This monster is also called a slime eel
* ✷ Can turn a 5-gal. (20-L) tub of water into slime in minutes

I am a pirate of the deep-sea floor, swooping in from out of the blackness to attack weak or sick individuals. Fearsome legends surround me—I am known to wiggle into an animal and eat it from the inside out!

My primitive "eyespots" sense light only vaguely. I can go for months without eating, so a whole whale carcass rotting on the ocean floor is my buried treasure! I have no jaws. Instead, I clamp on with toothy suckers that drag food down my throat. I have a disgusting habit of producing mucus that reacts with water to produce a thick slime. If I find myself in a tight spot, I loop my body into a knot that slips down from my head to my tail, ridding me of both my slime coating and my enemy in one *slick* maneuver.

* ● Longest hagfish: up to 50 in. (127cm) (*Eptatretus goliath*)
* ● Shortest hagfish: up to 7 in. (18cm) (*Myxine pequenoi*)
* ● "Eel-skin" wallets, purses, and handbags are actually made using hagfish skin

Hagfish

Sea Cucumber

■ Deep-down Dandies

- ✳ Simple echinoderm, related to starfish and sea urchins
- ✳ Herds of these invertebrate grazers cross deep-sea mud flats
- ✳ Makes up more than 90 percent of complex life in the inky ocean

I'm a very simple beast—essentially a squishy bag with leathery skin and a mouth at one end. I am at home on the ocean-floor mud plains. These stretch on forever— the largest habitat anywhere on Earth.

The most common creatures down here are the tiny guys that live off the organic debris falling from the ocean above. These tasty little beasties make up a large part of my diet, and I vacuum them up as I plow across the ocean floor. My simplicity is astounding—my coral-reef cousins can "liquefy" their bodies to pour themselves through cracks, reforming on the other side. I react to danger with gusto, quickly jettisoning my body parts out of my rear end. Hard to "stomach," I know, but it certainly distracts my attackers, and I can always regrow anything missing.

- ● Scientific name: Holothuroidea
- ● Average size: 4–12 in. (10–30cm) long
- ● Average life span: 5–10 years

Sea Cucumber

Hydrothermal Vent

■ Deep-down Dandies

- ✷ Hot, mineral-rich waters gushing out from the ocean floor
- ✷ Forms a chimney called a black or white "smoker"
- ✷ These fuming funnels are active only for a few decades

Angry, forbidding, and surrounded by swirling clouds of particles, I occur where Earth's tectonic plates are moving away from one another.

Seabed rocks are saturated with water. Below them, heat rises from deep inside the planet. It superheats the water circulating in the seabed, forcing it out of cracks to form my tall, mineral-rich chimneys. I am home to the only animals on Earth not sustained by energy from the Sun. There are strange blind crabs and shrimp, bright-red giant tubeworms, huge clams, and Pompeii worms—Earth's most heat-tolerant complex animal—sitting very comfortably in water as hot as 176°F (80°C) or as cool as 68°F (20°C).

- ● First discovery of a hydrothermal vent: 1977
- ● Tallest deep-sea vent chimneys: 200 ft. (60m) (Atlantic Ocean)
- ● Spreading center: the name for an area where Earth's plates are moving apart

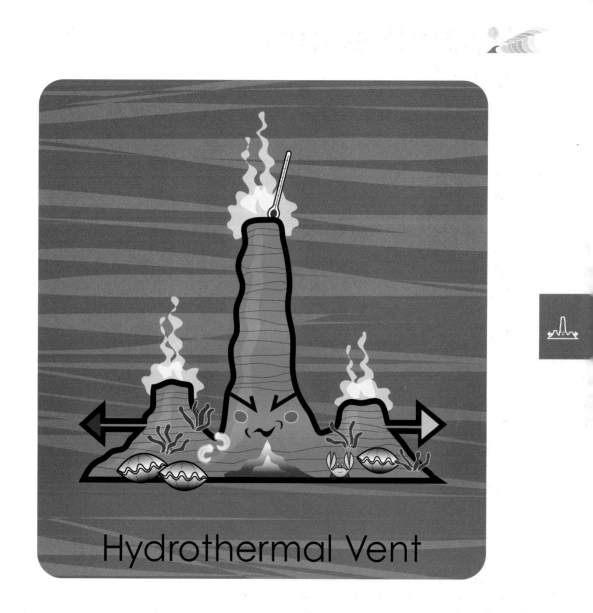

Hydrothermal Vent

CHAPTER 7

Frosty Fellows

Locked in ice for much of the year, the seas around Earth's poles are bleak places. Their chilled inhabitants have to be on their toes to keep from freezing their paws, fins, and flippers off! That is why they are a blubbery bunch, with layers of fat beneath their skin to keep them toasty in the cold water. You might think that the going would be too tough in these high latitudes, that animals would go in search of a more comfortable climate, but upwelling waters loaded with vital nutrients and yearly blooms of plankton keep the supplies full and the living good. The Frosty Fellows are here to make a splash!

Sea Ice

Ice Shelf

Krill

Ice Fish

Narwhal

Killer Whale

Walrus, Seal,
and Sea Lion

Polar Bear

Penguin

Sea Ice
Frosty Fellows

* Ice that is made when seawater freezes
* Formed at both poles, it makes up the polar ice packs
* "Fast ice" sticks to the coastline; "drift ice" floats around

I'm a drifter—I like to go with the *floe*. I appear when it gets cold enough for seawater to freeze. As it does so, it loses some of its salt content. Ice is less dense than liquid water, so I float on top of the sea, changing size with the seasons. I balloon in the winter and shrink with the summer melt. With each passing year, there's less of me around as the world's oceans heat up. Shame!

Sea Ice

● Freezing point of seawater: 28.8°F (−1.8°C)
● Total area of polar ice pack: 6 million sq. mi. (15.6 million km²)
● Thickness of pack ice: 3–13 ft. (1–4m)

Ice Shelf

Frosty Fellows

* Floating platform of ice that juts out into the sea
* Made of compressed snow, the ice is fresh water
* Large pieces of shelf snap off to float free as icebergs

Ice Shelf

A cold shoulder is all you'll get if you nestle up to me. Unlike my bro, Sea Ice, I form on land from snow that gets compressed into glaciers. I slip down to the shore as glacier ice and end up jutting out into the sea like a tuft of frozen water. Being compressed makes my ice denser than normal ice, and so almost 90 percent of me floats beneath the surface. Feel the chill!

- Thickness of sheet: 330–3,300 ft. (100–1,000m)
- Largest existing iceberg: Iceberg B-15—183 mi. (295km) long, 23 mi. (37km) wide
- An iceberg caused the *Titanic* to sink on her maiden voyage in 1912

Krill
Frosty Fellows

* Shrimplike crustaceans related to crabs and lobsters
* Like living in swarms of hundreds of millions of animals
* Main food source for many sea animals

Life is tough when you're snack food for half the animals in the ocean. We stick together in brain-boggling numbers, keeping a sharp lookout for whales, penguins, squids, seals, and many, many fish. Although we swim at only 2–4 in. (5–10cm) per second, we snap our tails when threatened and fire through the water—we're the ultimate fast food!

We spend our days avoiding predators, shivering in the cold and dark, 330 ft. (100m) below the surface. By night, we rise up as a vast cloudy mass to feed on microscopic phytoplankton. We have the largest biomass of any single creature on Earth—more than double that of humans and rivaled only by copepods (mini crustaceans to you). We're tiny but hugely important, and without us, life in the cold Southern Ocean simply wouldn't survive.

● Scientific name: *Euphasia superba*
● Average size: 2 in. (5cm)
● Distribution: Southern Ocean

Krill

Ice Fish
Frosty Fellows

* Group of closely related fish who live in Antarctic waters
* Can cope with temperatures as low as 28°F (–2°C)
* There are 122 known species to date

Brrr. I'd love to come in from the cold, but I have a mission to undertake in the subzero Southern Ocean: to survive! My cousins and I are specially equipped for the task. Some of us have handy antifreeze proteins in our blood. This prevents our bodies from freezing as we swim. Others have no red blood cells at all, and their thinner blood flows better in these chilly conditions.

Ice Fish

* Water temperatures that ice fish can endure: 28–39°F (–2–4°C)
* Maximum size: 6 in. (15cm) long
* Maximum life span: 15 years

Narwhal

Frosty Fellows

* Medium-size whale with a single, straight, spiraled tusk (males)
* One of the world's deepest-diving marine mammals
* Travels in pods of up to 20 members

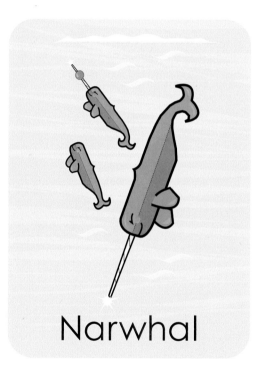

Narwhal

I'm an old sailor of the northern zone, an Arctic wanderer plying ancient routes under the sea ice. I can descend to 5,000 ft. (1,500m), where I cruise the sea floor hunting for fish, shrimp, and squids. My tusk is actually an extremely long left incisor tooth. I am hunted by Killer Whale, Polar Bear, and Inuit people—my blubber is their main source of vitamin C. Hey, get those guys some oranges!

● Average length: 13–20 ft. (4–6m)
● Tusk length: 7–10 ft. (2–3m)
● Distribution: Arctic waters around Greenland, Canada, and parts of Russia

Killer Whale
Frosty Fellows

- A highly intelligent hunter and member of the dolphin family
- A mean predator who travels in troops of ten to 20
- The male dorsal fin can be taller than a full-grown man

I'm a slick-skinned murderer—my other name, orca, means "from the dead." Any sea creature that sees my tall, black dorsal fin cutting toward it through the water had better say its prayers.

Trust me, I am one merciless beast. I target prey with my fellow henchmen, hunting and harassing them for hours. I'm super swift, snatching whale calves from their moms and drowning them. I terrorize whale sharks and have even suffocated great whites by holding them upside down. By bobbing upright in the water, I spot seal cubs sheltering on ice floes. I rock the floating platform or wash water over it to roll them into the water, and then I kill them with a tail slap. I'll even surge onto the shore and risk beaching myself to grab tasty sea-lion pups. It's a *killer*, I can tell you!

- Average size: 20–26 ft. (6–8m)
- Life span: up to 80 years
- Distribution: worldwide/all oceans, but prefer cold water

Killer Whale

Walrus, Seal, and Sea Lion
Frosty Fellows

* Triplet of fin-footed marine mammals called pinnipeds
* "Honk" to recognize and communicate with one another
* Give birth and raise their young on land

Meet the pinniped family, a bunch of barrel-shaped, blubbery flipper foots! Weighing more than 4,400 lb. (2,000kg), Walrus is instantly recognizable: think big tusks and mustache.

True seals are sleek-snouted, agile swimmers, and, boy, can we dive. During a dive, our hearts beat ten times slower than normal, shutting off the blood supply to nonessential parts. This allows us to stay underwater for longer, while a thick layer of insulating blubber keeps us warm. Our cousins, the sea lions and fur seals, are like us, but they have more doglike snouts and tiny ears. Their rear flippers can go back and forth to help them walk on land, while ours are more like a fishy tail—*flipper*ing useless out of the water!

* Scientific names: Odobenidae (walrus), Phocidae (seal), Otariidae (sea lion)
* Largest pinniped: southern elephant seal—up to 13 ft. (4m) long
* Endangered species: Steller sea lion, Hawaiian monk seal

Walrus, Seal, and Sea Lion

Polar Bear
Frosty Fellows

* This North Pole bear measures up to 10 ft. (3m) from tip to tail
* Hunts its prey on the sea ice
* Mother raises pups in the winter, going five months without food

Call me Nanook, my Inuit name—it has a nice ring to it. I'm a real heavyweight—Earth's largest land carnivore. Hang on, what's a land animal doing in this book?

My scientific name, *Ursus maritimus*, should give you a clue. You see, I'm a "maritime bear"—I spend most of my time at sea. Killing every five days, I hunt seals on pack ice and through ice floes. I can easily swim 112 mi. (180km), and I'm often spotted more than 60 mi. (100km) offshore. I'm really good at conserving heat: my black skin is kept warm by two layers of thick fur. The outer "guard hairs" are transparent but, in bulk, look white. I can smell a seal up to 1 mi. (2km) away, and I'll wait silently in the water until it surfaces . . . they always surface. I'll bash through 10 ft. (3m) of snow to get a pup in its lair. It's smashing work!

* Weight of an adult male: up to 1,800 lb. (800kg)
* Sprinting speed: up to 25 mph (40km/h)
* Distribution: the Arctic—Alaska, Canada, Russia, Greenland

Polar Bear

Penguin
Frosty Fellows

* Chubby Antarctic sea bird, fully adapted to life at sea
* Has a streamlined body, flipper wings, and heavy bones
* Incredibly powerful and balletic swimmer

I have you fooled! I'm no cute bird in a tuxedo—I'm an agile, two-tone ninja. Okay, so I get in a flap out of the water, but what do you expect? I'm squat, I waddle, and I can't fly. Get me *in* the water, though, and I'll go expertly in for the *krill*!

I'm a tough old thing, coming in to land on breakers that would snap a ship in two. Fortunately, I bounce off the rocks! My dark-top/light-belly combo makes me difficult to spot in the water. Thick, matted feathers and a blubbery layer keep me warm in freezing seas. When it comes to incubating eggs, none does it better than the male emperor, who balances an egg on his feet for more than two months. Hundreds of them huddle together to stay warm in vicious Antarctic storms. That's male bonding for you!

* Largest penguin: emperor penguin—up to 3.6 ft. (1.1m) tall
* Diving speed: 4–7 mph (6–12km/h)
* Distribution: Southern Hemisphere (mostly Antarctica)

Penguin

CHAPTER 8
Ocean Explorers

These intrepid explorers demonstrate some of the ways in which humans investigate and exploit the oceans. Life should be a beach for these adventurers—there are still many regions that are largely unexplored—but it seems that we humans have a beef with the blue stuff. While 3,000 robot probes surface every ten days to beam ocean data back to base, we are whisking food out of the water faster than it can be replaced. Meanwhile, no end of muck floats around, fouling open water and coastlines around the globe. And then there's ocean warming—the greatest threat of all. Time to throw Ocean a lifesaver!

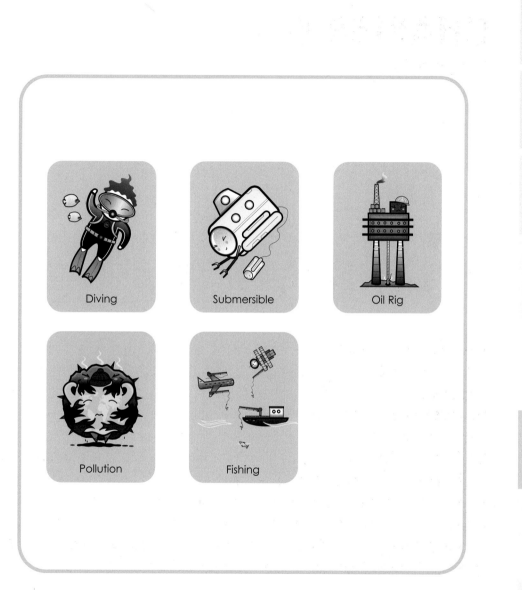

Diving

Submersible

Oil Rig

Pollution

Fishing

Diving
Ocean Explorers

* The main way to get a glimpse of the underwater world
* Specialist equipment allows exploration to greater depths
* Used for fishing, research, search and rescue, and pleasure

I'm pure excitement, a portal to a whole new universe. In my simplest form, I am one stage up from swimming. But there's more to me than that. Just take a deep breath, dip your head under, and you'll find out.

Many people "free dive," which involves holding your breath underwater to fish or for a competition. A snorkel tube and mask make this a little easier, while wearing flippers gives you additional power. Add an air tank and regulator and you have the scuba-diving equipment that frogmen use. Things get a little more complicated the farther down you go, with increasing pressure and decreasing temperatures. And diving is not without its dangers: humans can suffer from deadly, crippling cramps called "the bends" if they surface too quickly from the deep.

● Free-diving record (with fins): 869 ft. (265m) (Dave Mullins, 2010)
● Deepest-diving mammal: up to 2 mi. (3km) (sperm whale, up to 90 min. submerged)
● Average elephant seal dive: up to 1 hour

Diving

Submersible

■ Ocean Explorers

✳ Manned or not, this little fellow travels down to great depths
✳ Very sturdily constructed for a life under pressure
✳ Maintains atmospheric pressure for manned expeditions

Launched off the back of a research vessel, I travel deep into the inky depths. My strong, steel hull can cope with pressures that a human body could never withstand. If I'm not manned, I take the form of a robot explorer—a remotely operated vehicle (ROV). Some of my pals have descended to the bottom of Challenger Deep (35,840 ft., or 10,924m), the ocean's deepest point.

Submersible

● Submersibles that visited Challenger Deep : *Trieste*, *Kaiko*, and *Nereus*
● *Alvin*: submersible that discovered the first hydrothermal vent (1977)
● *Argo*: ROV that discovered the *Titanic* (1985)

Oil Rig

Ocean Explorers

- ✳ Roughneck who drills for fossil fuels on the ocean floor
- ✳ This artificial island is also known as an offshore platform
- ✳ Ranks among the world's biggest human-made objects

Oil Rig

The ocean bedrock often harbors fossil fuels and gas, and it's my job to extract them. You'll usually find me close to the shore, where it is easier to get the job done. Although I'm mostly submerged, I am taller than many skyscrapers. Life aboard me is very risky—drilling and storing flammable substances under pressure means that an outbreak of fire is a constant danger.

- ● World's deepest-drilling platform: Perdido Spar—9,627 ft. (2,934m), Gulf of Mexico
- ● World's largest platform: Hibernia platform—364 ft. (111m) high, Atlantic Ocean
- ● Deepwater Horizon oil spill: more than 20 million gal. (75 million L), 2010, Gulf of Mexico

Pollution

■ Ocean Explorers

✳ Litter, industrial waste, and sewage—all helping kill the sea
✳ Some are easy to spot (oil spills); others are invisible (sewage)
✳ Toxins accumulate and become concentrated in food chains

A dirty, sniveling bunch, we ride the waves as litter, oil spills, industrial waste, shipping waste, and raw sewage. Collectively, we are messing up the Big Blue—bigtime!

Litter, our most blatant member, forms unsightly plastic tangles on beaches. In open water, Ocean Current rounds it up into huge "garbage patches." Thick, gloopy oil slicks suffocate all life: zooplankton become deformed, sea birds can't fly, and fish and mammals can't breathe. The real evils are the invisible pollutants. Sewage stifles oxygen by encouraging microbial blooms, while leaks of heavy metals, toxins, and nuclear waste from industry can poison wildlife and even end up harming humans who eat polluted seafood. We're a mean bunch, and an encounter with any one of us can only end in disaster.

● Proportion of litter on beaches that is plastic: 50%
● Number of sea birds killed by plastic waste each year: up to one million
● Waste thrown into the Mediterranean Sea: 50 million tons per year

Pollution

Fishing

Ocean Explorers

* Global industry that takes fish from the sea
* Large-mesh nets are used to prevent overfishing
* Turtle-exclusion devices stop the netting of turtles

I have been reaping Ocean's spoils for many thousands of years. For much of this time, the waters were bursting with food that was awesomely good to eat. For all of the fish pulled out of the water, more grew to replace them.

Today, better technology and greater demand mean that I now outstrip Ocean's capacity to provide. I have gone high-tech! Thanks to spotter planes, satellite tracking, and sonar detection of schools of fish, fishermen now hit the jackpot every time. But don't be fooled. Cleaning up like this has a price. Even though the mighty cod can live to 20 or 30 years old, few of its kind in the North Atlantic ever get to this age now. Many are caught before they reach maturity, so they never become old enough to spawn and make new fish. And so the cycle goes on . . . not.

* Global fish capture: 99 million tons per year
* Number of people dependent on fishing: 450 million
* Top five commercial-fishing nations: China, Peru, Japan, United States, Chile

Fishing

INDEX

Character entries are **bold**

GLOSSARY

Alga (pl. algae) A simple, nonflowering plant without real roots, stem, or leaves; often single-celled.

Amphibious Describes a creature that can live in and out of water.

Biomass The total mass of animals (or plants) in an area, zone, or habitat.

Bivalve A type of mollusk, encased in two hinged shells (e.g., oyster, mussel, clam, and scallop), that attaches to rocks with strong, silky threads.

Blubber The layer of insulating fat under the skin of sea mammals and birds.

Brachiopod An invertebrate whose soft body is protected by two hinged shells that attach to rocks with a stalk.

Cartilage A tough and flexible connective tissue; some fish have skeletons made from cartilage.

Cephalopod Octopus, squid, and cuttlefish; a predatory mollusk with large eyes and tentacles surrounding a beaked mouth; squirts a cloud of inky fluid to confuse its predators.

Chelonian A group of reptiles that includes the turtle family, tortoises, and terrapins.

Clutch A group of eggs produced by a reptile.

Colony A community of animals living close together.

Continent Earth's main blocks of land (Africa, Asia, Antarctica, Australia, Europe, North and South America).

Copepod A small crustacean living as plankton; the most numerous animal on Earth.

Crustacean An invertebrate with a segmented body, jointed legs, and a hard outer shell called an exoskeleton (e.g., crab, lobster, barnacle, and copepod).

Cyclone A wind that moves in a circular motion toward an area of low pressure.

Detritus Organic remains, such as pieces of dead animals and plants, on which some sea creatures feed.

Echinoderm A marine invertebrate with a hard skeleton, tube feet, and a body shape based on a five-pointed star (e.g., starfish, sea urchin, and sea cucumber).

Floe A sheet of floating ice.

Gastropod A mollusk with a large muscular "foot" and a spiral shell (e.g., sea snail and whelk).

Herbivore An animal that feeds only on plants.

Hermaphrodite An animal with both male and female sexual organs.

Hydroid A tiny aquatic invertebrate with a tube body and a ring of stinging tentacles around the mouth.

Invertebrate An animal without a backbone.

Latitude Imaginary lines that divide Earth horizontally—high latitudes are zones near the poles; low latitudes are near the equator.

Mammal A warm-blooded animal, often with hair, that gives birth to live young.

GLOSSARY

Migration The seasonal journey made by an animal from one region to another.

Mollusk A member of a group of aquatic invertebrates that includes gastropods, cephalopods, and bivalves.

Monsoon A wind that changes direction with the seasons.

Multicellular Describes any life form with more than one cell.

Omnivore An animal that eats both plants and other animals.

Photosynthesis The process by which plants and algae use sunlight to turn carbon dioxide and water into food.

Pinniped A group of marine mammals, including seals, walrus, and sea lions).

Polyp A single member of a coral colony, a hydra, or a sea anemone.

Predator Any animal that hunts other animals.

Radiation (Sun's) Energy that comes from the Sun in the form of infrared waves, visible light, and ultraviolet waves.

Saline Describes water that is salty.

Siphon A tube through which sea animals suck things in or blow things out.

Sonar The sound waves used for echolocation (detecting objects underwater).

Tectonic plate A large chunk of Earth's crust that moves as one piece.

Venomous Describes an animal that carries poison and that can bite or sting.